ARGONAUT AND JUGGERNAUT

THE NEW READERS LIBRARY

*

ARGONAUT AND
JUGGERNAUT

OSBERT SITWELL

DUCKWORTH
3 HENRIETTA STREET
LONDON

First Published - - 1919
*Reissued in the New Readers
Library* - - - - 1927

"HOW SHALL WE RISE TO GREET THE DAWN?"

How shall we rise to greet the dawn,
Not timidly,
With a hand above our eyes?
We will welcome the strong light
Joyfully.
Nor will we mistake the dawn
For the mid-day.

We must create and fashion a new God—
A God of power, of beauty, and of strength—
Created painfully, cruelly,
Labouring from the revulsion of men's minds.

It is not only that the money-changers
Ply their trade
Within the sacred places;
But that the old God
Has made the Stock Exchange his Temple,
We must drive him from it.
Why should we tanker with clay feet?
We will fashion
A perfect unity
Of precious metals.

Let us tear the paper moon
From its empty dome.
Let us see the world with young eyes.
Let us harness the waves to make power,
And in so doing,

" HOW SHALL WE RISE TO GREET
THE DAWN ? "

How shall we rise to greet the dawn,
Not timidly,
With a hand above our eyes?
We will welcome the strong light
Joyfully?
Nor will we mistake the dawn
For the mid-day.

We must create and fashion a new God—
A God of power, of beauty, and of strength—
Created painfully, cruelly,
Labouring from the revulsion of men's minds.

It is not only that the money-changers
Ply their trade
Within the sacred places;
But that the old God
Has made the Stock Exchange his Temple.
We must drive him from it.
Why should we tinker with clay feet?
We will fashion
A perfect unity
Of precious metals.

Let us tear the paper moon
From its empty dome.
Let us see the world with young eyes.
Let us harness the waves to make power,
And in so doing,

Seek not to spoil their rolling freedom,
But to endow
The soiled and straining cities
With the same splendour of strength.

We will not be afraid,
Tho' the golden geese cackle in the Capitol,
In fear
That their eggs may be placed
In an incubator.
Continually they cackle thus,
These venerable birds,
Crying, " Those whom the Gods love
Dir young."
Or something of that sort.
But we will see that they live
And prosper.

Let us prune the tree of language
Of its dead fruit.
Let us melt up the clichés
Into molten metal ;
Fashion weapons that will scald and flay ;
Let us curb this eternal humour
And become witty.
Let us dig up the dragon's teeth
From this fertile soil
Swiftly,
Before they fructify ;
Let us give them as medicine
To the writhing monster itself.

We must create and fashion a new God—
A God of power, of beauty, and of strength ;
Created painfully, cruelly,
Labouring from the revulsion of men's minds.
Cast down the idols of a thousand years,
Crush them to dust
Beneath the dancing rhythm of our feet.
Oh ! let us dance upon the weak and cruel :
We must create and fashion a new God.

November, 1918.

CONTENTS

CONTENTS

PREFACE

BOOK I: THE PHOENIX-FEASTERS

Part I

BOOK II: GREEN-FLY

BOOK III: PROMENADES

BOOK IV : WAR POEMS

My thanks are due to Messrs. Blackwell for permission to reprint certain poems which first appeared in the anthology " Wheels," and to the editors of *The Times*, the *Nation*, *Art and Letters*, the *Cambridge Magazine*, *Everyman*, *Colour*, *New Paths*, and *Poetry and Drama* (New Series), for allowing me to reprint various poems which first appeared in their columns. Several of the war verses at the end of this volume first appeared in the *Nation* under the signature " Miles."

BOOK I

THE PHOENIX-FEASTERS

(*To* EDITH)

PART ONE

PRELUDE

WE have wandered through the dim valleys of sleep
—That lie so still and far—
Have bathed in the lakes of silence,
Where each star
Shines brighter than its own reflection in the heavens ;
Where, diving deep,
My soul has sought to catch and keep
The silver feathers of the moon
That float like down upon the waters,
In whose pale rest
We find
Forgetfulness of death
That comes so soon
—Waters that lull the mind
With some sweet breath
Of wind, of flowers,
With summer showers of rain,
Or quicken it with recreative pain.
We have fled further from this leaden cage,
Seeking those rainbow forests,

Where the light
Thrills through you, shaking, fainting, with delight;
Where sway tall luminous trees
Wind-swept in one vast flashing harmony,
That like a wave
Splashes its seething sound
And then envelops you.

We have strayed to other places,
Courts of fear,
That stretch like echoes through the endless dusk
Drenched with dead memories;
Like musk
They cling about you
In a heavy cloud.
Each shadow-sound we hear
Clutches the heart.
With fevered hands we tear
The terror-pulsing walls
—Fight our way out
—Out
Into other courts
As vague and full of fear.
And we have found the proud and distant palaces
        of night.

THE SILENCE OF GOD

One night upon the southern sea
In helpless calm we lay,
Waiting for day,
      Waiting for day.

As gold, ripe fruit fall from a tree
A comet fell; no other sight,
But in the ocean tracks of light
Trembled—then passed away,
      Away.

No sound broke on our waiting ears,
Though instinct whispered wayward fears
Of things we cannot tell—
      Of things the sea could tell.

No wisp of wind, no watery sound
Reached us; as if high on the ground
We stayed. A sense of fever fell
Upon each mind,
      Each soul and mind.

Until our eyes, that ever sought
The cloying, empty darkness, find
Another shape—or is it wrought
Of terror?—on the deep,
      The endless deep.

All dark it lay. No light shone out;
And though we cried across, no shout
Came back to us. As if in sleep
The black bulk lay so still,
      So still.

No sign came back ; no answering cry
Cleft the immense monotony
That swathed us like a funeral pall,
In folds of menace ; almost shrill
The silence seemed,
   And we so small.

Swiftly a boat was lowered down ;
The rowlocks creaked ; our track shone white
Behind us like God's frown,
   God's frown.

We clambered up that great ship's height ;
There was no light ; there was no sound ;
Nor was there any being found
Upon that ship,
   That sightless ship.

We groped our way along. God knows
How long the rats had been alone
With dust and rust ! Yet flight was shown
To have been instant, in the grip
Of some force stronger than its foes
   —Its human foes.

  * * * * *

Then, of a sudden, out there thrilled
The distant dying of a song
That hung like haze upon the sea, and filled
Each soul with joy and terror strong,
   With joy and terror strong.

Upon the sombre air were spent
These notes, as from a hidden place
Where all time and all love lay pent
In lingering embrace—
      In lingering embrace.

Deep in our hearts we felt the call;
We knew that if our fate should send
That song again, we must leave all
And follow to the end,
      The end.

ADVENTURE

DOWN through the torrid seas we swept,
Sails curved like bows about to shoot.
As an arrow speeds through the air,
Our ship parted the clinging waters.

Then, out of the ocean
Blossomed a distant land.

       *   *   *   *   *

The air quivered,
Dancing above it
In a frenzy of passion.
Waves of heat trembled towards us
Across the cool lassitude of the ocean.
They rolled new odours at us,
Sounding the chords of hidden senses,
Till we were alert
With minds as sensitive and taut
As resined strings.
The sea itself
Crouched down behind us,
Urging us on,
Driving us on,
To unknown
Perilous adventure.

       *   *   *   *   *

Ship and sea were forgotten.
We trampled
And stumbled
On, on,

Through the burning sand
To the hot shroud of the squat threatening forest,
Where, as you walked,
You tore apart
A solid sheet of air.

Brown satyrs grimaced at us,
Swinging with long hairy arms
From crooked branch to crooked branch.
The sun
Was at its height.
Rays pierced the hot shade ;
White lines of light
Shot through the shadows
To where a point of green
Shuddered with dangerous movement,
Throbbed and hummed with the whirr of insects.
Birds more bright than any streamers from the sun
Cleft the air
Like hammers ;
Scintillating wings
Tossed patches of colour
Into the dark shimmering air.
Shrill calls
Whistled like knives
Hurled through the empty heat.

Frantic chattering rose up
Through the honeycombéd darkness
Slim animals
—Their hides splashed with false sunlight—
Quivered away
Into the hollow distance,

Or clattered past us,
Cloven hooves
Kicking at the hard, bent trunks
Of gnarléd trees.
Large hairy fruits of wood
Were cast at us,
Snarlingly,
From the darkness.
Faces
—Faces peered down
From the interwoven boughs.

Hastily we stumbled on ;
Hurriedly we stumbled back,
Bewildered.
Small tracks
Tripped through the blackness
Hither and thither ;
Twigs crawled from under our feet,
Hissing away
In venom
—And we were bewildered.

Then suddenly
We felt,
Rumbling in curling patterns through the ground,
The beating of drums.
As winds bellow into caves,
As waves swirl and curl into hollows,
We heard the blowing of wooden trumpets
And of pipes.

Soon,
Under the western canopy of the sun,
Where the fevered hills lay huddled together,
We saw great gourd-shaped palaces
Loom up like mountains.
Figures played on trumpets,
Twisted like snakes,
Or on the curved, carved horns of unknown beasts.
In the sound was mirrored
The panic seizures of the night
—The fear of things that walk in darkness.
The drums were painted
In hot colours
That, even through the dusk,
Glowed torture and writhing torment.
Like a shower of molten lead
The din fell down upon us
From the Palaces.

Bare yellow women
Hurried
To greet us;
Their heels swayed inward
As they walked.
They offered fruits
—Fruits that were strange to us;
Mellow they were, and with a scent
Of sun, of summer,
And of woodland nights.
We ate
—And dreams closed round.

DUSK

NIGHT like a hawk
Swooped down
On to the phoenix bird,
—Tore out its flaming feathers.
Solitary plumes
Flared down into the darkness,
Floating above the distant sea.
Stillness and heat clung together
And the hawk
Spread out her wings.

Gigantic pinions
Flutter the air above,
Fanning our faces
And
We sing. . . .

SAILOR-SONG

ON swinging seas our ship has flown
—In sun and shadow lands alit.
We saw the sack of Carthage Town
(And Dido building it).

Cassandra, direful prophetess,
We heard foretell the fate of Troy,
And through its streets helped wheel and press
That wooden, painted toy.

We've seen events aboard this hulk
Of grave import and mystery
—The serpent's writhing horrid bulk
Go seething through the sea.

Then once we left Atlantis Town.
Behind us like a lily flower
It blossomed ; but then down, far down,
Sank veery vane and tower.

Now you can hear the clanging beat
Of bells beneath the furious foam.
In coral palaces the great
Sea monsters make their home :

Their corridors with pearl are pav'd ;
Float down them in an endless flight
Fierce finny beasts. The walls are laved
In iridescent light.

We brought gifts—myrrh and frankincense—
From Khubla to the Great Moghul ;
Espied the Juggernaut immense
Pound over flesh and skull ;

Saw desert-men atone for ills
With frenzied hands, with wounds that gape,
—The hermits hidden in the hills
—The Herod in his Tyrian cape.

From out our ship, held fast by gale,
We watched Andromeda's release ;
Beheld the galleon in full sail
That flew the Golden Fleece.

Icarus, proud of his new power,
We saw stretch out his wings to fly.
We heard in that tremendous hour
The cry from Calvary.

Thus many things we understand
That puzzle landsmen : we can tell
Of perils in each time and land ;
But outside Heaven or Hell

No fruit so strange we tasted save
But one ; none cast so strange a spell
Except the fruit the first Eve gave
To the first man who fell.

THE DANCE

THE song ends.
The rocking earth
Plunges madly
—Lunges like a man
About to fight.
Trees roll beckoning branches at us,
Branches that swing and sway.
From the forest
The animals
Howl
Like laughter.
With their burning scimitars
Flames slice the night.

Monotony,
A life preserved in ocean salt,
Scales off our limbs.
Within our veins
The liquor of this fruit-of-fire
Mounts in splendour inexhaustible.
The world itself
Dances
To make us dance
In cosmic frenzy.

WHY SHOULD A SAILOR RIDE
THE SEA?

WHY should a sailor ride the sea,
When he **can** drink and dance and sing,
Or watch the stars out-blossoming
Upon the tree of night?

Why should he face the tear-salt waves,
When he can sing, or feast on fruit,
Dance to the silver-sobbing lute,
And all men seem his slaves?

No more to ship or sea we'll go,
To watch the land sink out of sight
Suffused by purple fumes of night,
Each heart weighed down with woe,

But under rustling, fretted lace
Of leaves, we'll whirl and stamp our feet
And gesture to the furious beat,
—The rhythm of all space—

Or watch each dappled fawn and elf
Spring from the green lairs where they hide;
Now every soul is multiplied
And communes with itself.

The softly sailing moon is now
A pendulum, hung in a vast
Blue bubble—so to mark our fast
Lithe movements to and fro.

Down from the sky the willing stars
Fall round each brow a crown to form ;
Till feet and limbs, a rushing storm,
Dance whirling on in ecstasy.

The earth dances ;
The earth dances ;
Trees charge at us
Like horsemen ;
Forests swoop
Down the hill,
Charging at us,
But we are brave,
Full of a fiery courage,
And go onward
Onward,
Through the galloping trees.
We shout
Glowing phrases
—Snatches of ineffable wit.

The frenzy in our feet
Must surely set the world afire,
Yet still the stars
Rain down their golden tremors of delight,
And the moon
Sweeps like a bird
Through the arch of space.

We, too,
Float downward
Gently
To soft shipwreck.

We, too,
Are of the kindred of the Pleiades,
Reel on our golden path
Down,
Down,
Through the curvéd emptiness of the heavens.

THE PHOENIX-FEASTERS

PART TWO

CORNUCOPIA

Now music fills the night with moving shades;
Its velvet darkness, veinéd like a grape,
Obscures and falls round many a subtle shape
—Figures that steal through cool, tall colonnades,
Vast minotaurian corridors of sleep;
Rhythmic they pass us, splashed by red cascades
Of wine; fierce-flashing fountains, whose proud waves
Shimmer awhile, plunge foaming over steep
Age-polished rocks into the dim, cold caves
Of starlit dusk below—then merge with night,
Softly as children sinking into sleep.

But now more figures sway into our sight;
Strong and bare-shouldered, pressed and laden down,
Stagger across the terraces. They bear
Great cornucopia of summer fruit
And heavy roses scented with the noon
—Piled up with fruit and blossoms, all full blown,
Crimson, or golden as the harvest moon—
Piled up and overflowing in a flood
Of riches; brilliant-plumaged birds, that sing
With the faint playing of a far, sweet lute,
Warble their tales of conquest and of love;

Perch on each shoulder ; sweep each rainbow wing
Like lightning through the breathless dark above.
Heaped up in vases, gems shine hard and bright ;
Sudden they flare out—gleaming red like blood—
For now the darkness turns to ragged light ;
Great torches gild each shadow, tear the sky,
As drums tear through the silence of the night,
Breaking its crystal quiet—making us cry
Or catch our sobbing breath in sudden fear.
A shadow stumbles, and the jewels shower
On to the pavers with a sharp sweet sound,
To mingle with the fountain drops that flower
Up in a scarlet bloom above the ground,
A beauteous changing blossom ; then they rain
On to the broad, mysterious terraces,
Where sea-gods rise to watch in cold disdain
Before those vast, vermillion palaces,
—Watch where the slumbering coral gods of noon,
Drunk with the sudden golden light and flare
Of flaming torches, try to pluck and tear
That wan enchanted lotus flower, the moon,
Down from its calm still waters ; thus they fall,
Like flowing plumes, the fountains of our festival.

Slowly the torches die.   They echo long,
These last notes of a Bacchanalian song,
Of drifting, drowsy beauty, born of sleep,
—Vast as the sea, as changing and as deep.
In thanksgiving for shelt'ring summer skies
Still, far away, a fervent red light glows.
Small winds brush past against our lips and eyes,
Caress them like a laughing summer rose,
And rainbow moths flit by, in circling flight.

A harp sobs out its crystal syrupings ;
Faintly it sounds, as the poor petal-wings,
Fragile yet radiant, of a butterfly
Beating against the barriers of night.

Then from the Ocean came the Syren song,
Heavy with perfume, yet faint as a sigh,
Kissing our minds, and changing right from wrong ;
Chaining our limbs ; making our bodies seem
Inert and spellbound, dead as in a dream.

        *   *   *.   *   *

Bound by the silver fetters of your voice
To this new slavery of dreams,
We, listening, rejoice.
The magic strains
Swell in this darkness star-devoid.
The music streams
Upon the world in patterns passionate yet clear,
And stains
Each soul. The mind, decoyed
By thoughts that grind and tear
Away old values,
Is sent down other thoughts
So subtly swift,
That in their fleeting passage
They can cut adrift our souls
Upon a sea of wonder and of fear.
Within the arid minds of men
This music sounds but once, for then
They hear no other song.
In it, tumultuous rush of wings,
The glamour of old, lovely things

In deserts buried long,
The grace of beasts that bound and leap
With movements blithe and strong
—Of those that creep
Away in hissing-reptile rage—
All these, all these are found.
They hear
The secrets, solved, of each dead age,
Each mystery is clear.
For in this music's flow, the din
Of spheres that tear and speed and spin
Through pulsing space is heard,
And all things men have loved and feared
Are mirror'd in each sound.

SONG

OUR hidden voices, wreathed with love's soft flowers,
Wind-toss'd through valleys, tremble across seas
To turban d cities ; touch tall, lonely towers,
Call to you through the sky, the wind, the trees.

Misted and golden as the hanging moon,
That like a summer fruit floats from the sky,
Thrills out our distant, age-enchanted tune,
—Nor will it let you pass our beauty by.
But if it should not reach to stir your mind,
Then hold a summer rose against the ear,
Till through its crimson sweetness you can hear
The falling flow of rhythm—so designed
That from this secret island, like a star
Shining above a shrouded world, our song
Cleaves through the darkest night and echoes long,
Bidding you follow whether near or far.
Come hither where the mermaids churn the foam,
Lashing their tails across the calm, or dive
To groves and gardens of bright flowers, then roam
Beneath the shadow of stone trees, or drive
Some slow sea-monster to its musselled home.
Here, as a ladder, they climb up and down
The rainbow's steep, refracted steps of light,
Till, when the dusk sends down its rippling frown,
They quiver back to us in silver flight.
The moon sails down once more ; our mermaids
          bring
Rich gifts of ocean fruit.   Again we sing.
Enchantment, love, vague fear, and memories
That cling about us like the fumes of wine

C

With myriad love-enhancing mysteries
We pour out in one song—intense—divine,
Down the deep, moonlit chasms of the waves
Our song floats on the opiate breeze. Why seek
To goad your carven galleys, fast-bound slaves
Who search each sweeping line of bay and creek,
Only to stagger on a hidden rock, or find
The limp, dead sails swept off by sudden wind ?
Thus always you must search the cruel sea,
For if you find us, mankind shall be free !

But when you sleep we grasp you by the hand,
And to the trickling honey of the flute
We lead you to a distant, shimmering land
Where lotus-eaters munch their golden fruit,
Then fall upon the fields of summer flowers
In drunken sunlit slumber, while a fawn
Prances and dances round them.
                                          Oh, those hours
When through the crystal valleys of the dawn
Down from the haunted forests of the night
There dash the dew-drenched centaurs on their way,
Mad with the sudden rush of golden light
—Affright the lotus-eaters, as they sway
Towards the woodlands in a stumbling flight.
In those deep groves we follow through the cool
Shadow of high, columnar trees, to find
The fallen sky within a forest pool
Now faintly veiled and fretted by a wind,
Lest our white flashing limbs should turn you blind.

*   *   *   *   *

As the sweet sound of bells that fall and fade
In watery circles on the verge of night,
So rounded ripples spread beneath the shade
Of flowing branches dripping with green light.

Thus do we wander ; but when day is spent
We grope our way through vast tall palaces,
Palaces sinister and somnolent,
Where lurk dim fears and unknown menaces.

These high, pale walls and this pale, shining floor
Seem built of bones, by ages planed and ground
To a white smoothness.
                    On this rock-bound shore
The bodies of dead sailors oft are found.

These sombre arches pierce the sullen sky.

These pillars are the pillars of the night.

Of what avail your strife and agony ?
Why seek to search and struggle for the light ?
Our music chains you : binds your limbs from flight.

PROSPECT ROAD

GIGANTIC houses, tattered by all time,
Raise their immense and ruined bulk and height
In one unending universal street,
Against a strange and sunken yellow sky
—Like sunset trickling through into the sea,
Down to the depths, yellow and grey and green.
Blind windows face the interminable road ;
Innumerable those windows seem to stretch
All smeared and stained and stamped with time and
        blood,
—Stains that seem faces—horrid twitching masks
Moving their lewd, derisive lips and tongues,
Spitting out treacheries with vampire lips—
Or eyes that gaze from far blank-stretching walls
—The tortured eyes of those who see their death
Approaching aeon-by-aeon along this road.
Behind the walls sound voices whispering
Of dire and hidden, carefully hidden, thoughts—
Cruel, wicked and unfathomable things
That lie behind this infamy of stone.
Then clamour, shrieking voices, or a pause
That falls like lead through the suspended air ;
Broken by laughter—rending piercing sounds
That seem to tear the fabric of our minds.
Slinking along these wicked, stricken walls,
I reached a shining, distant point of light.
And glory came—vast and unending light,
Rays—flashing, writhing rays of light.
And then the music sounded. Ah, that sound !

Cadences rose and fell unendingly—

Quivering, shining waves of sound and sight—
Sounds of the universe—the cries of space
And planets tumbling wildly round our world
—Showing the meaning of the meaningless.
" God and eternity "—strange flashing sounds
The whirl of time, " Melchisedec "—" Glory of God "
And space—the universe—like framing words—
" Gog and Magog "—" Infinity "—the rush of waters
And the sky comes down.
                    Down with the splintering stars.

1916-1919.

BOOK II

GREEN FLY

WAR-HORSES

How they come out
—These Septuagenarian Butterflies—
After resting
For four years

Surely they are more spirited
Than ever ?
Their enamelled wings
Are rusty with waiting,
Their eyelids
Sag a little,
Like those of a bloodhound,
But they swim gaily into the limelight.

Oh, these war-horses,
They have seen it through !
Theirs has been a splendid part,
The waiting and the weariness :
For the Queens of Sheba
Are used to courts and feasting ;
But for four years
Platitudes have remained
Uncoined,

For there have been few parties
And only
Three stout meals
A day.

But now
They have come out.
They have preened
And dried themselves
After their blood-bath.
Old men seem a little younger,
And tortoise-shell combs
Are longer than ever;
Earrings weigh down aged ears;
And Golconda has given them of its best.

They have seen it through!
Theirs is the triumph,
And, beneath
The carved smile of the Mona Lisa,
False teeth
Rattle
Like machine guns,
In anticipation
Of food and platitudes.
Oh! les Vieilles Dames Sans Merci!

CHURCH-PARADE

THE flattened sea is harsh and blue—
Lies stiff beneath—one tone, one hue,
While concertina waves unfold
The painted, shimmering sands of gold.

Each bird that whirls and wheels on high
Must strangle, stifle in, its cry,

For nothing that's of Nature born
Should seem so on the Sabbath morn.

The terrace glitters hard and white,
Bedaubed and flecked with points of light

That flicker at the passers-by—
Reproachful as a curate's eye.

And china flowers, in steel-bound beds,
Flare out in blues and flaming reds ;

Each blossom, rich and opulent,
Stands like a soldier ; and its scent

Is turned to camphor in the air.
No breath of wind would ever dare

To make the trees' plump branches sway,
Whose thick green leaves hang down to pray.

The stiff, tall churches vomit out
Their rustling masses of devout,

Tall churches whose stained, Gothic night
Refuses to receive the light!

Watch how the stately walk along
Toward the terrace, join the throng

That paces carefully up and down
Above a cut-out, cardboard town!

With prayer-book rigid in each hand,
They look below at sea and sand,

The round contentment in their eyes
Betrays their favourite, fond surmise,

That all successful at a trade
Shall tread eternal Church-Parade,

And every soul that's sleek and fat
Shall gain a heavenly top-hat.

From out the Church's Gothic night,
Past beds of blossoms china-bright,
Beneath the green trees' porous shade,
We watch the sea-side Church-Parade.

AT THE HOUSE OF MRS. KINFOOT

At the house of Mrs. Kinfoot
Are collected
Men and women
Of all ages.
They are supposed
To sing, paint, or to play the piano.
In the drawing-room
The fireplace is set
With green tiles
Of an acanthus pattern.
The black curls of Mrs. Kinfoot
Are symmetrical.
—Descended, it is said,
From the Kings of Ethiopia—
But the British Bourgeoisie has triumphed.
Mr. Kinfoot is bald
And talks
In front of the fireplace
With his head on one side,
And his right hand
In his pocket.
The joy of catching tame elephants,
And finding them to be white ones,
Still gleams from the jungle-eyes
Of Mrs. Kinfoot,
Though her mind is no jungle
Of Ethiopia,
But a sound British meadow.

Listen, then, to the gospel of Mrs. Kinfoot :
" The world was made for the British Bourgeoisie,

They are its Swiss Family Robinson;
The world is not what it was.
We cannot understand all this unrest!

Adam and Eve were born to evening dress
In the southern confines
Of Belgravia.
Eve was very artistic, and all that,
And felt the fall
Quite dreadfully.
Cain was such a man of the world
And belonged to every club in London;
His father simply adored him,
—But had never really liked Abel,
Who was rather a milk-sop.
Nothing exists which the British Bourgeoisie
Does not understand;
Therefore there is no death
—And, of course, no life.

The British Bourgeoisie
Is not born,
And does not die,
But, if it is ill,
It has a frightened look in its eyes.

The War was splendid, wasn't it?
Oh, yes, splendid, splendid."

Mrs. Kinfoot is a dear,
And so artistic.

GREEN-FLY

I.

LIKE ninepins, houses stand up square
  In lines; their windows mouths to bite
At servants, who lean out to stare
  At anything that moves in sight.

Where once was green-limbed tree or ledge
  Of greener moss or flowery lane,
Set back behind a private hedge
  Each house repeats itself again.

Each house repeats itself again,
  But smaller still and yet more dry;
For—just as those who live within—
  So have these houses progeny.

Throughout each dusty endless year,
  Whose days seem merely wet or fine,
These children constantly appear
  In an unending, dusty line.

As on a rose that is ill-grown
  Nature, insulted and defied,
Showers down a blight, so sends she down
  On houses, those who live inside.

II.

Within each high, well-papered room,
  Compressed, all darkness lay,
Darkness of night, and crypt, and tomb,
  Nor ever entered day.

But through the endless black there crept,
  With groping hand and groping thought,
With eyes that blinked, but never wept,
  And minds that fell, but never fought,

The wonderless, the hard, the nice,
  Who scurry at a ray of light,
Then, like a flock of frightened mice,
  Career back into night.

From out this damning, dreadful dark
  (While history, thundering, rolls by)
They wait for an anæmic lark
  To sing from weak blue sky.

Or if a dog is hurt, why then
  They see the evil, and they cry.
But yet they watch ten million men
  Go out to end in agony !

Their own strange God they have set up,
  Of clay, of iron, and mothéd hide ;
Whose eyes, each convex as a cup,
  Reflect the herd endeified.

Their twisted feet in boots He made
  To walk the narrow asphalt way,
And gave each room a curtain's shade
  To muffle out the light of day.

For this God understands their need ;
  Creates the lid for each pale eye ;
He scoops each mouth to say " Agreed,"
  And gives them coffins when they die.

Then, if for punishment they go
    To other lands, oh, let it be
Their judgment that, down there below,
    They see this world as they might see!

A world of contrast, shade and light—
    Clashing romance and cruelty,
But stricken with the dreadful blight
    Of fear to feel and fear to cry.

Where for a moment lives are filled
    With love or hate—where born of pain
The children grow up—to be killed.
    Where freedom—dead—is born again.

Wherein life's pattern crude and shrill
    Is weft by neither foe nor friend,
But by some rough, colossal will
    Towards some vast, invisible end.

But in those houses dark there creep,
    With bodies wrapt in woollen dress,
With eyes that blink but never weep,
    The sentimental wonderless!

DE LUXE

I.

HYMN.

ABOVE from plaster-mountains,
  Wine-shadowed by the sea,
Spurt white-wool clouds, as fountains
  Whirl from a rockery.

These clouds were surely given
  To keep the hills from harm,
For when a cloud is riven
  The fatted rain falls warm.

Through porous leaves the sun drops
  Each dripping stalactite
Of green. The chiselled tree-tops
  Seem cut from malachite.

Stiff leaves with ragged edges
  (Each one a wooden sword)
Are carved to prickly hedges,
  On which, with one accord,

Their clock-work songs of calf-love
  Stout birds stop to recite,
From cages which the sun wove
  Of shade and latticed light.

Each brittle booth and joy-store
  Shines brightly. Below these
The ocean at a toy shore
  Yaps like a Pekinese.

II.

Nursery Rhyme.

The dusky king of Malabar
Is chief of Eastern Potentates ;
Yet he wears no clothes except
The jewels that decency dictates.

A thousand Malabaric wives
Roam beneath green-tufted palms ;
Revel in the vileness
That Bishop Heber psalms.

From honey-combs of light and shade
They stop to watch black bodies dart
Into the sea to search for pearls.
By means of diabolic art

Magicians keep the sharks away :
Mutter, utter, each dark spell,
So that if a thief should steal,
One more black would go to Hell.

But Mrs. Freudenthal, in furs,
From brioche dreams to mild surprise
Awakes ; the music throbs and purrs.
The cellist, with albino eyes,

Rivets attention ; is, in fact,
The very climax ; pink eyes flash
Whenever nervous and pain-racked
He hears the drums and cymbals clash.

Mrs. Freudenthal day-dreams
—Ice-spoon half-way to her nose—
Till the girl in ochre screams,
Hits out at the girl in rose.

This is not at all the way
To act in large and smart hotels;
Angrily the couples sway,
Eagerly the riot swells.

Girls who cannot act with grace
Should learn behaviour; stay at home;
A convent is the proper place.
Why not join the Church of Rome?

A waiter nearly drops the tray
—Twenty tea-cups in one hand.
Now the band joins in the fray,
Fighting for the Promised Land.

Mrs. Freudenthal resents
The scene; and slowly rustles out;
But the orchestra relents,
Waking from its fever bout.

BOOK III

PROMENADES

NOCTURNE

THE valleys that were known in sunlit hours
Are vast and vague as seas;
Wan as the blackthorn flowers
That quiver in the first spring-scented breeze
Far as the frosted hollows of the moon.
The sighing woods are still—
Wrapp'd in their age-long boon
Of mystery and sleep. A naked hill,
Loud and discordant, looms against the sky,
And little lights like stars
Break the monotony
Of blue and silver, black and grey. Strange bars
Of light resemble silver masks, and leer
Across the forest lane.
Tall nettles, rank from rain,
Scent all the woods with some ancestral fear.

Trees rustle by the water. A voice sings
Faintly, to ward off fright.

The water breathes pale rings
Of sad, wan light;
Faintly they grow,
Then merge into the night:
The last poor twisted echo takes to flight.

THE LAMENT OF THE MOLE-CATCHER

To W. H. DAVIES

AN old, sad man who catches moles
　　Went lonely down the lane—
All lily-green were the lanes and knolls,
　　But sorrow numbed his brain.
He paid no heed to flower or weed
　　As he went his lonely way.
No note he heard from any bird
　　Who sang, that sad spring day.

" I trap'd the moles for forty years.
　　They could not see the sky.
I reckoned not blind blood or tears,
　　And the Lord has seen them die.
For forty years I've sought to slay
　　The small, the dumb, the blind,
But now the Lord has made me pay,
　　And I am like their kind.
I cannot see or lane or hill,
　　Or flower or bird or moon ;
Lest life shall lay me lower still,
　　O Lord—come take it soon."

THE BEGINNING

GREAT spheres of fire, to which the sun is naught,
Pass thund'ring round our world. A golden mist—
The margin to the universe—falls round
The verges of our vision. Rocks ablaze
Leap upward to the sun, or fall beneath
The rush of our rapidity, that seems
Catastrophy, and not the joyous birth
Of yet another star. The air is full
Of clashing colour, full of sights and sounds
Too plain and loud for men to heed or hear,
The cosmic cries of pain that follow birth :
A multi-coloured world.

                  The scorching heat
Surpasses all the equatorial days :
Steam rises from the surface of the sea.
Gigantic rainbow mists resemble forms
That bring to mind strange elemental sprites
Exulting in the chaos of creation.
They glide above the tumult-ridden sea
Which now is shaken as are autumn leaves ;
Great hollows open and reveal its depths—
Devoid of any form of life or death.
Till wave on wave it gathers strength again
And shakes a mountain, splits it to the base
(Still weak from struggle as a new-born babe).
Then night comes on, and shows the flaming path
Of all the rocks that vainly seek the sun.
Broad as the arch of space, a myriad moons
Sail slowly by the sea ; the glowing world
Shows up the pallor of their ivory.
The din grows greater from the universe :

There rises up the smell of fire and iron—
Not dreary like the smell of burnt-out things,
But like the smell of some gigantic forge—
Cheerful, of good intent, and full of life.

Now all the joyous cries of sea and earth,
The universal harmonies of birth,
Rise up to haunt the slumber of their God.

THE END

ROUND the great ruins crawl those things of slime ;
Green ruins, lichenous and scarred by moss—
An evil lichen that proclaims world doom,
Like blood dried brown upon a dead man's face.
And nothing moves save those monstrosities,
Armoured and grey, and of a monster size.

But now, a thing passed through the cloying air
With flap and clatter of its scaly wings—
As if the whole world echoed from some storm.
One scarce could see it in the dim, green light
Till suddenly it swooped and made a dart
And brushed away one of those things of slime,
Just as a hawk might sweep upon its prey.

It seems as if the light grows dimmer yet—
No radiance from the dreadful green above,
Only a lustrous light or iridescence
As if from off a carrion-fly—surrounds
That vegetation which is never touched
By any breeze. The air is thick, and brings
The tainted, subtle sweetness of decay.
Where, yonder, lies the noisome river-course,
There shows a faintly phosphorescent glow.
Long writhing bodies fall and twist and rise,
And one can hear them playing in the mud.
Upon the ruined walls there gleam and shine
The track of those grey, vast monstrosities—
As some gigantic snail had crawled along.

All round the shining bushes waver lines
Suggesting shadows, slight and grey, but full
Of that which makes one nigh to death from fear.

Watch how those awful shadows culminate
And dance in one long wish to hurt the world.

A world that now is past all agony !

FOUNTAINS

'The graven fountain-masks suffer and weep.
Carved with a smile, the poor mouths clutch
At a half-remembered song,
Striving to forget the agony of ever laughing."
                                SACHEVERELL SITWELL.

SOME fountains sing of love
In full and flute-like notes that charge the night
With all the red-mouthed essence of the rose ;
Then turn to voices murmuring above,
Among the trees,
Of hidden sweet delight.

Another fountain flows
With the faint music of a first spring breeze ;
Each falling drop is jewelled by the moon
To some fine luminous ecstasy of light.
It sings of noon,
Of sunlit blossoms on a first spring day
And all things sweet and pleasant to the sight.

Another fountain sings
Of the cool pleasures of those moonlit hours
When dappled sylvan things
Trample through thickets and through secret bowers
To prance and play,
Or, squatting round in rings,
To wreathe their hornéd heads with wan, sweet
          flowers
Till dawn comes grey and sweeps them to the wood.

Another fountain sobs
Its song of passions that have passed away.
Then with a sound like threatening, rolling drums,
      it throbs
And bursts into a flood
Of fierce wild music ; and its savage spray
Becomes the blood
Renewed, of crimes long past.

Another fountain sings its song of fear,
Of rustics flying fast
Before some foe—
A deadly, unknown foe that comes so near
They feel his panting breath,
And run for many a lengthy, panic mile.

Those graven fountain-masks are white with woe !
Carved with a happy smile
They strive to weep . . .
End their eternal laughing—for awhile
To lose themselves in sleep,
Or in the silver peacefulness of death.

SONG OF THE FAUNS

WHEN the woods are white beneath the moon
And grass is wet with crystal dew,
When in the pool,
So clear and cool,
The moon reflects itself anew,
We raise ourselves from daylight's swoon,
We shake away
The sleep of day,
Out from our bosky homes we spring ;
Horns wreathed with flowers,
Throughout the hours
Of moonlight, worshipping we sing.
Pale ivory goddess, whose wan light
Looks down upon us worshipping—
Each dappled faun
Who shuns the dawn,
Is here, and rarest gifts we bring—
The feathers of the birds of night
Wrought to a crown
Of softest down
We offer you, and crystal bright,
The dew within a lily cup
Reflecting stars
In shining bars ;
All things most strange we offer up—
Rich gifts of fruit and honeyed flowers
To place within your secret bowers.
We shake down apples from the trees,
And pears, and plums with velvet skin ;
Up to the sky
We cast these high

And pray you'll stoop to net them in.
We dance : then fall upon our knees
And pray and sing—all this to show
The love that all loyal fauns must owe
To you, white goddess of the night.
But no more play,
We must away,
The eastern sky is growing bright.

" A SCULPTOR'S CRUELTY "

THE faun runs through the forest of the noon,
  Then leaps into some lovely, shrouded glade
  Splashed with hot light.   He dances in the shade
Of tower-like trees, whose branches sway and swoon
  Beneath their weight of green.   No breath of air
Ruffles the vivid blossom or the moss
  On which he pirouettes, all is so fair !

He leaps about ; then, tired and at a loss
  For what to do, he roams the wood—espies
A figure like himself—but stiff and grey,
  Lacking the hairy chest and dappled thighs
That are his pride.   " But surely this can play
  And scamper, dance and snuffle through the day
As well as me ? "   So he comes near and eyes
  The lichened features of a faun of stone.

  Oh ! it is sad to be so young—alone !

PIERROT OLD

THE harvest moon is at its height,
The evening primrose greets its light
With grace and joy: then opens up
The mimic moon within its cup.
Tall trees, as high as Babel tower,
Throw down their shadows to the flower—
Shadows that shiver—seem to see
An ending to infinity.

Now Pan, the pagan, has unbent
And stoops to sniff the night-stock scent
That brings a memory sad and old,
When he was young, and free, and bold,
And played his pipe in forests black,
Or followed in some goatherd's track
Who, fill'd with panic fear, still flees
Through all the terror-threatening trees.

Huge silver moths, like ghosts of flowers,
Hover about the warm dark bowers,
And wait to breathe the lime-tree scent
That perfum'd many a compliment
Address'd to beauties young and gay,
Their faces powdered by the ray
Of that same moon that looks upon
Their dreary, lichen-cover'd tomb.
The nyads throw their water wide
And strive to stem the surging tide
That dashes up the fountain base,
Hoping to catch the moon's pale face—

A game now played without a score
For three good centuries or more.
And all the earth smells warm and sweet
—A fitting place for fairy feet.

But now a figure white and frail
Leaps out into the moonlight pale.
From wakeful thoughts, old age and grief,
He finds in this strange world relief.
Yet all the shadow, scent and sound,
Poor Pierrot's mind do sad confound.
Watch how he dances to the moon
While singing some faint, fragrant tune !

But Pierrot now is tired and sad
—Remembers all the evenings mad
He spent with that fantastic band
So gaily wand'ring o'er the land.
They all are dead—and at an end,
And he is left without a friend.
For tho' the hours can pass away,
Poor Pierrot still must grieve and stay.

Upon the dewy grass he lies :
The perfumes stir strange memories.
Once more he hears a laughing cry
That brings great tear-drops to his eye.
That step—that look—that voice—that smile.
Ah ! they've been buried a long while !
And who's the man in pantaloons,
And he who sings such festive tunes ?
Why, it's that laughing man of sin,
That roguish rascal Harlequin !

Forgiving Pierrot hides his head
Deep in the grass and mourns the dead;
Forgetting all the pranks they play'd,
And how he was himself betray'd.

The butterfly lives but one day,
But Pierrot still seems doom'd to stay.

He falls asleep there, tragic-white,
And wakes to find the bleak daylight.

NIGHT

ALL the dim terrors dwelling far below,
Interr'd by many thousand years of life,
Arise to revel in this evil dark :
The wail forlorn of dogs that mourn for men—
A shuffling footfall on a creaking board,
The handle of a door that shakes and turns—
A door that opens slightly, not enough :
The rustling sigh of silk along a floor,
The knowledge of being watched by one long dead,
By something that is outside Nature's pale.
The unheard sounds that haunt an ancient house :
The feel of one who listens in the dark,
Listens to that which happened long ago,
Or what will happen after we are dust.
The awful waiting for a near event,
Or for a crash to rend the silence deep
Enveloping a house that always waits—
A house that whispers to itself and weeps.
The murmur of the yew, or woodland cries,
A sombre note of music on the breeze ;
A shudder from the ivy that entwines
The horror that is felt within its grip.
The sound of prowling things that walk abroad,
The nauseous flapping of Night's bat-like wings—
These are the signs the gods have given us
To know the limit of our days and powers.

FROM CARCASSONNE

To MARGARET GREVILLE

I

Now night,
        The sighing night,
Descends to hide and heal
The crimson wounds
Ripped in the sky,
Where the high helmet-towers
(With clouds as streaming feathers)
Have torn the Heavens
In their incessant sunset battle.

Below,
        Upon the mound,
Small golden flowers
Release their daylight slowly
At the Night's behest,
Till they become pale discs
That quiver
When the evening wind
Draws his thin fingers
Down the dew-drenched grass
—As an old harper,
Who awakes
From drunken sunlit slumber,
Blindly plucks
His silver-sounding strings—
Making the sound
That, further, darker down
The trees make,
When they draw back
Their upturned leaves
In fountain-foaming hurry.

The curling, hump-backed dolphins,
Drunk with purple fumes
Of wine-stained sunset,
Plunge through the wider waters of the night—
Waters that well down every narrow street
In darkening billows,
Till they become quiet, full—
Canals that, mirror-like,
Reflect each sound
Of snarling song
In all the town.

And, as the dolphins dive,
There splashes back
Upon their goat-eared riders,
Dislodged in sudden fury,
The foaming froth of summer-cooling winds
—Issuing from where the northern trees
Bellow their resined breath
Across the seas
To ripple through far fields
Of twilight flowers—
Sweeping across
To where these old high towers
Of Carcassonne
Still stand to break their flow.

Neptune, from his high pedestal,
Can watch the waters of the night
Rise, further, further,
And the faun-riders sink below
The conquering, cool tide.

PROGRESS

THE city's heat is like a leaden pall—
Its lowered lamps glow in the midnight air
Like mammoth orange-moths that flit and flare
Through the dark tapestry of night. The tall
Black houses crush the creeping beggars down,
Who walk beneath and think of breezes cool,
Of silver bodies bathing in a pool,
Or trees that whisper in some far, small town
Whose quiet nursed them, when they thought that
        gold
Was merely metal, not a grave of mould
In which men bury all that's fine and fair.
When they could chase the jewelled butterfly
Through the green, bracken-scented lanes, or sigh
For all the future held so rich and rare ;
When, though they knew it not, their baby cries
Were lovely as the jewelled butterflies.

THE RETURN OF THE PRODIGAL

I LAY awake in that dim room of fear
Which seemed to hold the essence of the night,
Clutched in the grip of its tall sentient walls :
Dark walls and high, that stretch for ever up—
Up to the darkness, vague and menacing,
As if no light could ever penetrate
That mist of shadows, only cast a gloom
More cavernous upon the atmosphere
That seems to thicken into cloudy shapes,
Who gather substance and then fade and die ;
And all the room is full of whisperings ;
Of moving things that hope I do not heed ;
And sudden gusts of wind blow cold upon
My head, lifting the heavy mantle of the air,
Revealing for an instant some vague thought
Snatched from the haunting lumberland of dreams.
Far in the distance, from the open night,
Sounds an insistent hooting from the wood ;
The owl is calling to its kindred things.
The bat emits its sinful, piercing note—
So high one cannot hear it, only feel
The rhythm beat within the shrinking ear.
A faint breeze blows in from the countryside,
Rustling the curtains with the forest's breath,
Stirring the grass of many an unknown tomb,
Some new—and some immemorably old,
Whose dwellers never heard an owl at night,
Only the reptile sounds and beating wings
Of some forefather of that bird of night—
Some flapping, scaly monster with huge wings.
Then, sudden, through the rustling of the room

Silence shrills out its startling trumpet call
Of terror, and the house is frozen still.
Despair dropp'd down like rain upon my heart,
Catching my breath and clutching at my throat.
Fear magnified my senses, and my brain
Could hear beyond the threshold of this world.
Then through the threatening silence of the house,
This silent waiting for the coming play—
There came that halting, well-remembered tread,
The dreadful limp, and dragging of the feet;
That cruel sin-white face looked through the door!
And in my scream—that rent the trembling air,
Reaching the woods and tainting them with death,
Filling the fountain with strange ripplings
That make the moon's reflection but a mask
Like to that face of shame—my soul passed out—
Out of my ashen lips, to find its end.

LONDON SQUARES

To-night this city seems delirious. The air
Is fever'd, hot and heavy—yet each street,
Each tortuous lane and slumb'ring stone-bound
      square
Smells of the open woods, so wild and sweet.
Through the dim spaces, where each town-bred tree
Sweeps out, mysterious and tall and still,
The country's passionate spirit—old and free—
Flings off the fetters of the calm and chill.

There in the garden, fauns leap out and sing—
Chant those strange sun-born songs from far away!
With joyous ecstasy in this new spring,
They cast the coats and top-hats of the day.

There by the railings, where the women pace
With painted faces, passionless and dead,
Out of the dark, Pan shows his leering face,
Mocks their large hats and faces painted red.
Then as they walk away, he taunts their lives,
Racking each wearied soul with lost desires,
And—cruelty more subtle—he contrives
With aching memories of love's first fires
To tune their hearts up to a different key.
So, when they sleep the withered years unfold
—Again, as children round a mother's knee
They listen to their future as foretold
—A future rich and innocent and gay.

Then wake up to the agony of day!

TEARS

SILENCE o'erwhelms the melody of Night,
Then slowly drips on to the woods that sigh
For their past vivid, vernal ecstasy.
The branches and the leaves let in the light
In patterns, woven 'gainst the paler sky
—Create mysterious gothic tracery
Between those high dark pillars, that affright
Poor weary mortals who are wand'ring by.

Silence drips on the woods like sad faint rain
Making each frail, tired sigh a sob of pain ;
Each drop that falls, a hollow, painted tear
Such as are shed by Pierrots when they fear
Black clouds may crush their silver lord to death.
The world is waxen ; and the wind's least breath
Would make a hurricane of sound. The earth
Smells of the hoarded sunlight that gave birth
To the gold-glowing radiance of that leaf
Which falls to bury from our sight its grief.

CLAVICHORDS

To Violet Gordon-Woodhouse

Its pure and dulcet tone
So clear and cool
Rings out—though muffled by the centuries
Passed by ;
Each note
A distant sigh
From some dead, lovely throat.

A sad cascade of sound
Floods the dim room with faded memories
Of beauty that has gone,
Like the reflected rhythm in some dusk-blue pool,
Of dancing figures (long laid in the ground)—
Like moonlit skies
Or some far song harmonious and sublime—
Breaking the leaden slumber of the night.
A perfume, faint yet fair
As of an old press'd blossom that's reborn
Seeming to flower alone
Within the arid wilderness of Time.

The music fills the air
Soft as the outspread fluttering wings
Of flower-bright butterflies
That dive and float
Through the sweet rose-flushed hours of summer
    dawn.
The rippling sound of silver strings
Break o'er our senses as small, foaming waves

Break over rocks,
And into hidden caves
Of silent waters—never to be found—
Waters as clear and glistening as gems.

And in this ancient pool of melodies,
So soothing, deep,
We search for strange lost images and diadems
And old drowned pleasures,
—Each one shining bright
And rescued from the crystal depths of sleep.

As the far sun-kissed sails of some full-riggéd boat,
Blown by a salt, cool breeze,
—Laden with age-old treasures
And rich merchandise—
Fade into evening on the foam-flecked seas—
So this last glowing note
Hovers awhile—then dies.

PROMENADES

Long promenades against the sea
Kaleidoscopic, chattering!
Pavilions rising from the sea,
On which a fawning, flattering,
Hot crush of orientals move,
And sell their cheap and tawdry wares,
To other Jews, and aldermen,
And rich, retired, provincial mayors.
Oh! many colours in the sun;
Copper and gold predominate!
Parasols, held 'gainst the sun
Throw down their shadows inchoate
On leering faces looking sly—
All shining with the heat of June.
The shifting masses move and talk
And whistle tunes all out of tune.

Long promenades against the sea,
And oranges and mandolines!
Pavilions rising from the sea
And penny-in-the-slot machines!

CLOWN PONDI

WHEN youth and strength had changed my blood
to fire
And every day passed long and glorious,
Another link in the eternal chain
Of life, I turned my love of luring and my sense
For all the unfathomable ways of God,
My burning sense for laughter and my joy
In crowds, in tumult, and in blazing lights,
To make my fellows see these qualities.
Thus I became " Clown Pondi," and my fame
Grew high in every theatre in the land.

I seem'd to draw fresh vigour from the crowds—
Loving the sea of faces, eyes with tears,
And gaping mouths wide open—loosely hung ;
The acrid, opalescent haze of smoke,
Hanging above the auditorium.
And over it the crowded galleries
That float far up, like painted prows of ships—
All overweighed and alive with men.
I loved the limelight, hard and white and strong,
The throbbing music and the theatre's scent,
That artificial, paper, printed scent
That sweeps across the footlights to the stalls.

Then was I pleased to strut about the stage,
With face dead white, and strangely purple nose—
Flamboyant in the garb of foolery—
To run about too quickly—and fall down ;

To make queer noises—inarticulate
    Strange sounds and oaths, the signal for my share
Of cackling laughter.
                 Thus the years pass'd by
And—all unheeding—swept away my youth,
    Till, one sad night, I heard a voice near-by :
" Ah ! Poor old man ! It's shocking they should
       laugh ;
    Mock his bent legs, and poor old toothless jaws ! "

And then old-age rush'd down upon my head,
    Each sombre year roll'd past in solemn time ;
In true perspective—to the jingling tune
    That was my exit ; and so near came death,
Holding a mirror to my ridicule,
    That show'd each line beneath the smearing paint,
Each wrinkle underneath the dab of rouge,
    That in my sudden hopelessness I wept.

But as I left the stage with dragging feet,
    With body bent with age, and crouching low,
I heard the applauding people pause and say,
    " Who but Clown Pondi could amuse us so ? "

LAUSIAC THEME

SERAPION-THE-SINDONITE
Wore a cloth about his loins.
This Christian Recondite
Never carried coins:

Never did he ask for bread;
Revelled in his own distress,
High of spirit, low of head,
With no other dress

Than a loin-cloth. Serapion
Was free from greed and gluttony;
Progressed in the direction
Of impassivity.

Serapion, though ascetic,
Could not keep within his cell—
Spiritual athletic,
Who wrestled with Hell—

This Sindonitic holy man
Converted, overcome by pity,
Thais, the famous courtesan,
To Christianity.

Thais was not thin or frail,
But full of figure. Flesh and blood
Rose up in riot—made her rail
At a selfless God.

From Theban windows, far above,
She plays and sings to a guitar
With low voice : the light of love
Beckons like a star.

Eagerly she welcomed in
The unexpected Sindonite ;
But he spoke to her of sin—
Set her soul alight.

So they went together out
To the crowded, garish street,
Where he taught her how to flout
Fumes of wine and meat.

To the Thebaid they go—
Where she stands each Christian test,
Plaiting palm-leaves to and fro,
Sure of heaven's rest.

In the desert they both died,
Thais and the holy man.
They were buried side by side,
Ascetic and courtesan.

METAMORPHOSIS

THE woods that ever love the moon, rest calm and
      white
Beneath a mist-wrapp'd hill :
An owl, horned wizard of the night,
Flaps through the air so soft and still ;
Moaning, it wings its flight
Far from the forest cool,
To find the star-entangled surface of a pool,
Where it may drink its fill
Of stars ; a blossom-laden breeze
Scatters its treasures—each a fallen moon
Among the waiting trees—
Bears back the faded shadow-scents of noon.

The whispering wood is full of dim, vague fears.
The rustling branches sway
And listen for some sound from far away—
A silver piping down the Pagan years
Since Time's first joyous birth—
The listening trees all sigh,
The moment of their hornéd king is nigh.
Then, peal on peal, there sounds the fierce wild mirth
Of Pan their master, lord and king,
And round him in a moonlit ring
His court, so wan and sly !

But then the trees closed round and hid from sight
Their deeds—the voices seemed to die.

An owl, horned wizard of the night,
Flaps through the air so soft and still.
Moans, as it wings its flight
Toward the mist-wrapp'd hill.

THE GIPSY QUEEN

A RAGGED Gipsy walked the road,
Her eyes blazed fierce and strong,
She gazed at me as on she strode,
She fiercely gazed, and long.

" Give me a penny, sir," she said,
" To buy me drink and buy me bread,
For I've nothing had to eat or drink,
And at night I never sleep a wink.
Cold is the snow and wet the rain,
But my soul died when my love was slain ! "

" Fair Gipsy, in some southern clime,
I've seen your face before
In some far other distant time,
But whom are you weeping for ? "

" 'Twas Antony I loved," she said,
" For him, in vain, I shed these tears,
But my loved Antony is dead—
Is dead these long two thousand years ;
Then I was mighty Egypt's pride,
Fear'd both by friend and foe—

Yet they believe Cleopatra died
Two thousand years ago ! "

BLACK MASS

THE atmosphere is charged with hidden things
—Thoughts that are waiting—wanting to revive
Primeval terrors from their present graves
—Those half-thoughts hidden from the mind of man.

The fear of those bright, countless stars that shine
Celestially serene on summer nights,
—And those, too far for human eye to see—
That make men feel as small and ill at ease
As do the thoughts of immortality;
The fear of seas that stretch beyond our sight
Unspoilt by any memory of a ship—
Strange, silent seas that lap the unknown shores
Of some far-distant, undiscovered land;
The curious fear of caves and horrid depths
Where lurk those monsters that we hide away
And bury in our self-complacency.
The dread of all that waits unseen, yet heard;
The fear of moonlight falling on a face;
The sound of sobs at night, the fear of laughter;
The misty terror lurking in a wood
Which night has wrapped in her soft robe of sighs.
The horror that is felt where man is not,
In lonely lands all dotted with squat trees
That seem to move in the grey twilight breeze
—Or sit and watch you like malicious cripples,
Intent on every movement, every thought—
Where stones, like evil fungi, raise their bulk
Cover'd with lichen older than the hills—
A warning for the ages yet to come;
Stones that have seen the sun, and moon, and stars,
Deflect their course for very weariness.

These fears are gathered, press'd into a room
Vibrating with the wish to damage man ;
To put a seal upon his mind and soul—
These fears are fused into a living flame.

The room is filled with men of evil thought,
And some poor timid ones, on evil bent.
They stand in anxious, ghastly expectation.

The guttering light is low, and follows them
With subtle shadows, tall beyond belief :
Vast elemental shapes that make men feel
Like dusty atoms blown by wayward winds
About the world : shadows that sway and swing,
And sigh and talk, as if themselves alive.
Small shadows cringe about the room incredibly,
Grotesque and dwarf-like in their attitudes ;
Malignant, mocking things that caper round—
Triumphant heralds of an evil reign.
Secret and swift they flit about the wall ;
Noiseless, they drag their feet about the floor,
And murmur subtle infamies of love,
Sweet-sounding threats, and bribes, and baleful
        thoughts.

Yet all are waiting, evilly alert . . .
Yet all are waiting—watching for events.

Silence has ceased to be a negative,
Becomes a thing of substance—fills the room
And clings like ivy to the listening walls.
The flickering light flares up—then gutters out.
The shadows seem to shiver and expand
To active, evil things that breathe and live.

But now they whirl and dance in ecstasy.
The highest moment of their mass is near.
We only feel the swaying of the shades,
—Rhythm of wicked music that escapes
Our consciousness, tho' we have known it long—
The music of the evil things of Night
Scarcely remembered from some dim, vast world—
The things that haunted us when we were young
And nearer to our past realities.
Like scaly snakes, the hymn to evil writhes
Through the sub-conscious basis of our mind.
Eddies of icy breath, or hot as flame,
Twist into all the corners of the room,
Filling our veins with fire like red-hot iron,
And wicked as the Prince of Evil Things.

Faintly his glowing presence is revealed to us
Amid the chorus of his satellites.
The consummation of our awful hopes.

PIERROT AT THE WAR

THE leaden years have dragged themselves away;
   The blossoms of the world lie all dash'd down
And flattened by the hurricane of death:
The roses fallen, and their fragrant breath
   Has passed beyond our senses—and we drown
Our tragic thoughts: confine them to the day.

Pierrot was happy here two years ago,
   Singing through all the summer-scented hours,
Dancing throughout the warm, moon-haunted night.
Swan-like his floating sleeves, so long and white,
   Sailed the blue waters of the dusk.   Wan flowers,
Like moons, perfumed the crystal valley far below.

But now these moonlit sleeves lie on the ground,
   Trampled and torn from many a deadly fight.
With fingers clenched, and face a mask of stone,
He gazes at the sky—left all alone—
   Grimacing under every rising light:
His body waits the peace his soul has found.

April, 1917.

SPRING HOURS

THE air is silken—soft and dark—
Calm as the waters of some blue, far sea;
Sweet as a youthful dream,
The trees stand cold and stark,
Yet full of the new life which makes each tree
To tremble with delight; sets free
  The summer rapture of the stream.

But now the clouds disperse and drift away,
  Splashing the woods with patches of pale light,
Sail off like silver ships, and then display
  The dazzling, myriad blossoms of the night.

Ah! It is worth full many a sun-gilt hour
To see the heavens bursting into flower.

BOOK IV

WAR POEMS

"THEREFORE IS THE NAME OF IT CALLED BABEL"

AND still we stood and stared far down
Into that ember-glowing town,
Which every shaft and shock of fate
Had shorn unto its base. Too late
  Came carelessly Serenity.

Now torn and broken houses gaze
On to the rat-infested maze
That once sent up rose-silver haze
  To mingle through eternity.

The outlines once so strongly wrought,
Of city walls, are now a thought
Or jest unto the dead who fought . . .
  Foundation for futurity.

The shimmering sands where once there played
Children with painted pail and spade
Are drearly desolate—afraid
  To meet night's dark humanity,

Whose silver cool remakes the dead,
And lays no blame on any head
For all the havoc, fire, and lead,
  That fell upon us suddenly,

When all we came to know as good
Gave way to Evil's fiery flood,
And monstrous myths of iron and blood
    Seem to obscure God's clarity.

Deep sunk in sin, this tragic star
Sinks deeper still, and wages war
Against itself; strewn all the seas
With victims of a world disease
—And we are left to drink the lees
Of Babel's direful prophecy.

January, 1916.

TWENTIETH-CENTURY HARLEQUINADE

FATE, malign dotard, weary from his days,
Too old for memory, yet craving pleasure,
Now finds the night too long and bitter cold
—Reminding him of death—the sun too hot.
The beauty of the universe he hates,
Yet stands regarding earthly carnivals :
The clatter and the clang of car and train,
The hurrying throng of homeward-going men,
The cries of children, colour of the streets,
Their whistling and their shouting and their joy,
The lights, the trees, the fanes and towers of churches,
Thanksgiving for the sun, the moon, the earth,
The labour, love, and laughter of our lives.

He thinks they mock his age with ribaldry.

From far within his aeon-battered brain
Well up those wanton, wistful images
That first beguiled the folk of Bergamo.
Now like himself, degraded and distress'd,
They sink to ignominy ; but the clown
Remains, reminder of their former state,
And still earns hurricanes of hoarse applause.
This dotard now decides to end the earth
(Wrecked by its own and his futility).
Recalls the formula of world-broad mirth
—A senseless hitting of those unaware,
Unnecessary breaking of their chattels.

The pantomime of life is near its close :
The stage is strewn with ends and bits of things,

With mortals maim'd or crucified, and left
To gape at endless horror through eternity.

The face of Fate is wet with other paint
Than that incarnadines the human clown :
Yet still he waves a bladder, red as gold,
And still he gaily hits about with it,
And still the dread, revealing limelight plays
Till the whole sicken'd scene becomes afire.
Antic himself falls on the funeral pyre
Of twisted, tortured, mortifying men.

March, 1916.

THIS GENERATION

To HELEN

THEIR youth was fevered—passionate, quick to drain
    The last few pleasures from the cup of life
Before they turn'd to suck the dregs of pain
    And end their young-old lives in mortal strife.
They paid the debts of many a hundred year
    Of foolishness and riches in alloy.
They went to death ; nor did they shed a tear
    For all they sacrificed of love and joy.
Their tears ran dry when they were in the womb,
For, entering life—they found it was their tomb.

1917.

SHEEP-SONG

To FRANCIS MEYNELL

FROM within our pens,
Stout built,
We watch the sorrows of the world.
Imperturbably
We see the blood
Drip and ooze on to the walls.
Without a sigh
We watch our lambs
Stuffed and fattened for the slaughter. . . .

In our liquid eyes lie hidden
The mystery of empty spaces,
All the secrets of the vacuum.

Yet we can be moved;
When the head-sheep bleats,
We bleat with him;
When he stampedes,
Heavy with foot-rot
We gallop after him,
Until
In our frenzy
We trip him up
—And a new sheep leads us.

We are the greatest sheep in the world,
There are no sheep like us.
We come of an imperial bleat;
Our voices,
Trembling with music,
Call to our lambs oversea.
With us they crash across continents.

We will not heed the herdsmen,
For they warned us,
" Do not stampede " ;
Yet we were forced to do so.
Never will we trust a herdsman again.

Then the black lamb asked,
Saying, " Why did we start this glorious Gadarene
        descent ? "
And the herd bleated angrily,
" We went in with clean feet,
And we will come out with empty heads.
We gain nothing by it ;
Therefore
It is a noble thing to do.
We are stampeding to end stampedes.
We are fighting for lambs
Who are never likely to be born.
When once a sheep gets its blood up
The goats will remember. . . ."

But the herdsman swooped down
Shouting,
" Get back to your pens there."

September, 1918.

THE POET'S LAMENT

BEFORE the dawning of the death-day
My mind was a confusion of beauty.
Thoughts fell from it in riot
Of colour,
In wreaths and garlands of flowers and fruit. . . .

Then the red dawn came
—And no thought touched me
Except pity, anger
And bitter reproach.
God filled my mouth
With the burning pebbles of hatred,
And choked my soul
With a whirl-wind of fury.
He made my tongue
A flaming sword
To cut and wither
The white soft edges
Of their anæmic souls.
I ridiculed them,
I despised them,
I loathed them
. . . But they had stolen my soul away.
Yes, they had stolen my soul from me.
My heart jumps up into my mouth
In fury;
They have stolen my soul away.

But we will wait,
And later words will come
—Words that in their burning flight
Shall scorch and flay,

Or flare like fireworks
Above their heads.
In those days my soul shall be restored to me,
And they shall remember,
They shall remember !

JUDAS AND THE PROFITEER

JUDAS descended to this lower Hell
    To meet his only friend—the profiteer—
Who, looking fat and rubicund and well,
    Regarded him, and then said with a sneer,
" Iscariot, they did you ! Fool ! to sell
    For silver pence the body of God's Son,
Whereas for maiming men with sword and shell
    I gain at least a golden million."

But Judas answered : " You deserve your gold ;
It's not His body but His soul you've sold ! "

RHAPSODE

To H. W. Massingham

WHY should we sing to you of little things—
You who lack all imagination ?
Why should we sing to you of your poor joys,
That you may see beauty through a poet's mind—
Beauty where there was none before ?
Why should we heed your miserable opinions,
And your paltry fears ?
Why listen to your tales and narratives—
Long lanes of boredom along which you
Amble amiably all the dull days
Of your unnecessary lives ?
We know you now—and what you wish to be told :
That the larks are singing in the trenches,
That the fruit trees will again blossom in the spring,
That Youth is always happy ;
But you know the misery that lies
Under the surface—
And we will dig it up for you !
We shall sing to you
Of the men who have been trampled
To death in the circus of Flanders ;
Of the skeletons that gather the fruit
From the ruined orchards of France ;
And of those left to rot under an Eastern sun—
Whose dust mingles with the sand
Of distant, strange deserts,
And whose bones are crushed against
The rocks of unknown seas ;
All dead—dead,
Defending you and what you stand for.

You hope that we shall tell you that they found their
        happiness in fighting,
Or that they died with a song on their lips,
Or that we shall use the old familiar phrases
With which your paid servants please you in the
        Press :
But we are poets,
And shall tell the truth.

You, my dear sir,
You are so upset
At being talked to in this way
That when night
Has coffin'd this great city
Beneath the folds of the sun's funeral pall,
You will have to drink a little more champagne,
And visit a theatre or perhaps a music-hall.
What you need (as you rightly say, my dear sir) is
        CHEERING-UP.
There you will see vastly funny sketches
Of your fighting countrymen ;
And they will be represented
As those of whom you may be proud,
For they cannot talk English properly,
Or express themselves but by swearing ;
Or perhaps they may be shown as drunk.
But they will all appear cheerful,
And you will be pleased ;
And as you lurch amiably home, you will laugh ;
And at each laugh
Another countryman will be dead !

When Christ was slowly dying on that tree—
Hanging in agony upon that hideous Cross—

Tortured, betrayed, and spat upon,
Loud through the thunder and the earthquake's roar
Rang out
Those blessed humble human words of doubt:
" My God! My God! why hast Thou forsaken
    Me ? "
But near by was a cheerfully chattering group
Of sects,
Of Pharisees and Sadducees,
And all were shocked—
Pained beyond measure.
And they said:
" At least he might have died like a hero
With an oath on his lips,
Or the refrain from a comic song—
Or a cheerful comment of some kind.
It was very unpleasant for all of us—
    But we had to see it through.
I hope people will not think we have gone too far—
Or behaved badly in any way."

There in the street below a drunken man reels home,
And as he goes
He sings with sentiment:
" Keep the home fires burning ! "
And the constable helps him on his way.
    But we—
    We should be thrown into prison,
Or cast into an asylum,
For we want—
            PEACE !

September, 1917.

THE MODERN ABRAHAM

To SIEGFRIED SASSOON

His purple fingers clutch a large cigar—
  Plump, mottled fingers, with a ring or two.
He rests back in his fat armchair. The war
  Has made this change in him. As he looks
      through
His cheque-book, with a tragic look he sighs :
  " Disabled Soldiers' Fund " he reads afresh,
And through his meat-red face peer angry eyes—
  The spirit piercing through its mound of flesh.

They should not ask me to subscribe again !
  Consider me and all that I have done—
I've fought for Britain with my might and main ;
  I make explosives—and I gave a son.
My factory, converted for the fight
  (I do not like to boast of what I've spent),
Now manufactures gas and dynamite,
  Which only pays me seventy per cent.
And if I had ten other sons to send
I'd make them serve my country to the end,
So all the neighbours should flock round and say :
  " Oh ! look what Mr. Abraham has done.
He loves his country in the elder way ;
  Poor gentleman, he's lost another son ! "

1917.

THE TRAP

THE world is young and green.
Its woods are golden beneath the May-time sun ;
But within its trap of steel the rabbit plunges
Madly to and fro.
It will bleed to death
Slowly,
    Slowly,
Unless there is some escape.
Why will not someone release it ?

And presently a kindly passer-by
Stoops down.
The rabbit's eye glints at him—
Gleaming from the impenetrable obscurity of its
    prison.
He stoops and lifts the catch
(He cannot hold it long, for the spring is heavy).
The rabbit could now be free,
But it does not move ;
For from the darkness of its death-hutch
The world looks like another brightly baited trap.
So, remaining within its steel prison,
It argues thus :
" Perhaps I may bleed to death,
But it will probably take a long time,
And, at any rate,
I am secure
From the clever people outside.
Besides, if I did come out now
All the people who thought I was a lion
Would see, by the trap-mark on my leg,

That I am only an unfortunate rabbit,
And this might promote disloyalty among the
    children.
When the clamp closed on my leg
It was a ruse
To kill me.
Probably the lifting of it betrays the same purpose !
If I come out now
They will think they can trap rabbits
Whenever they like.
How do I know they will not snare me
Again next year ?
Besides, it looks to me from here . . . "

But the catch drops down,
For the stranger is weary.
From within the hutch
A thin stream of blood
Trickles on to the grass
Outside,
And leaves a brown stain on its brightness.
But the dying rabbit is happy,
Saying :
" I knew it was only a trap ! "

April, 1918.

THE ETERNAL CLUB

To RODERICK MEIKLEJOHN

WARMING their withered hands, the dotards say:
" In our youth men were happy till they died.
What is it ails the young men of to-day—
  To make them bitter and dissatisfied ? "

Two thousand years ago it was the same :
  " Poor Joseph ! How he'll feel about his son !
I knew him as a child—his head aflame
  With gold.   He seemed so full of life and fun.
And even as a young man he was fine,
Converting tasteless water into wine.
Then something altered him.   He tried to chase
  The money-changers from the Temple door.
  White ringlets swung and tears shone in their poor
  Aged eyes.   He grew so bitter and found men
For friends as discontented—lost all count
  Of caste—denied his father, faith, and then
He preached that dreadful Sermon on the Mount !
  But even then he would not let things be ;
  For when they nailed him high up on the tree,
  And gave him vinegar and pierced his side,
  He asked God to forgive them—still dissatisfied ! "

HEAVEN

A THEATRE rises dark and mute and drear
  Among those houses that stand clustering round.
Passing this pleasure-house, I seem'd to hear
  The distant rhythm of some lauding sound,
The hot applause that greeted every night
The favourite song, or girl, or joke, or fight.
  The laughter of the young and strong and gay
  Who greeted life—then laid their lives away.

Do they, then, watch the same old blatant show,
  Forgetting all death's wrench and all its pain
And all their courage shown against the foe ?
  Is this the heaven that they died to gain ?

THE BLIND PEDLAR

I STAND alone through each long day
Upon these pavers; cannot see
The wares spread out upon this tray
—For God has taken sight from me!

Many a time I've cursed the night
When I was born. My peering eyes
Have sought for but one ray of light
To pierce the darkness.   When the skies

Rain down their first sweet April showers
On budding branches; when the morn
Is sweet with breath of spring and flowers,
I've cursed the night when I was born.

But now I thank God, and am glad
For what I cannot see this day
—The young men crippled, old, and sad,
With faces burnt and torn away;

Or those who, rich and old,
Have battened on the slaughter,
Whose faces, gorged with blood and gold,
Are creased in purple laughter!

January, 1919.

WORLD-HYMN TO MOLOCH

Holy Moloch, blessed lord,
Hatred to our souls impart.
Put the heathen to the sword,
Wound and pierce each contrite heart.
Never more shall darkness fall
But it seems a funeral pall;
Never shall the red sun rise
But to red and swollen eyes.
In the centuries that roll,
Slowly grinding out our tears,
Often thou hast taken toll;
Never till these latter years
Have *all* nations lost the fray;
Lead not thou our feet astray.
Never till the present time
Have we offered all we hold,
With one gesture, mad, sublime,
Sons and lovers, lands and gold.
Must we, then, still pray to thee,
Moloch, for a victory?

Eternal Moloch, strong to slay,
Do not seek to heal or save.
Lord, it is the better way
Swift to send them to the grave.
Those of us too old to go
Send our sons to face the foe,
But, O lord! we must remain
Here, to pray and sort the slain.

In every land the widows weep,
In every land the children cry.
Other gods are lulled to sleep,
All the starving peoples die.
What is left to offer you ?
Thou, O Sacred King of Death !
God of Blood and Lord of Guile,
Do not let us waste our breath,
Cast on us thy crimson smile.
Moloch, lord, we pray to thee,
Send at least *one* victory.

All the men in every land
Pray to thee through battle's din,
Swiftly now to show thy hand,
Pray that soon one side may win.
Under sea and in the sky,
Everywhere our children die ;
Laughter, happiness and light
Perished in a single night.
In every land the heaving tides
Wash the sands a dreadful red,
In every land the tired sun hides
Under heaps and hills of dead.
In spite of all we've offered up
Must we drink and drain the cup ?
Everywhere the dark floods rise,
Everywhere our hearts are torn.
Every day a new Christ dies,
Every day a devil's born.
Moloch, lord, we pray to thee,
Send at least *one* victory.

1917.

ARMCHAIR

IF I were still of handsome middle-age
I should not govern yet, but still should hope
To help the prosecution of this war.
I'd talk and eat (though not eat wheaten bread),
I'd send my sons, if old enough, to France,
Or help to do my share in other ways.
All through the long spring evenings, when the sun
Pursues its primrose path toward the hills,
If fine, I'd plant potatoes on the lawn;
If wet, write anxious letters to the Press.
I'd give up wine and spirits, and with pride
Refuse to eat meat more than once a day,
And seek to rob the workers of their beer.
The only way to win a hard-fought war
Is to annoy the people in small ways,
Bully or patronize them, as you will!
I'd teach poor mothers, who have seven sons
—All fighting men of clean and sober life—
How to look after babies and to cook;
Teach them to save their money and invest;
Not to bring children up in luxury
—But do without a nursemaid in the house!

If I were old, or only seventy,
Then should I be a great man in his prime.
I should rule army corps; at my command
Men would rise up, salute me, and attack
—And die. Or I might also govern men
By making speeches with my toothless jaws,
Chattering constantly; and men should say,
" One grand old man is still worth half his pay! "

That day I'd send my grandsons out to France
—And wish I'd got ten other ones to send
(One cannot sacrifice too much, I'd say).
Then would I make a noble, toothless speech,
And all the listening Parliament would cheer.
" Gentlemen, we will never end this war
Till all the younger men with martial mien
Have entered capitals ; never make peace
Till they are cripples, on one leg, or dead !"
Then would the Bishops go mad with joy,
Cantuar, Ebor, and the other ones,
Be overwhelmed with pious ecstasy.
In thanking Him we'd got a Christian—
An Englishman—still worth his salt—to talk,
In every pulpit they would preach and prance ;
And our great Church would work, as heretofore,
To bring this poor old nation to its knees.
Then we'd forbid all liberty, and make
Free speech a relic of our impious past ;
And when this war is finished, when the world
Is torn and bleeding, cut and bruised to death,
Then I'd pronounce my peace terms—to the poor !
But as it is, I am not ninety yet,
And so must pay my reverence to these men—
These grand old men, who still can see and talk,
Who sacrifice each other's sons each day.
O Lord ! let me be ninety yet, I pray.
Methuselah was quite a youngster when
He died.   Now, vainly weeping, we should say :
" Another great man perished in his prime ! "
O let me govern, Lord, at ninety-nine ! "

August, 1917.

RAGTIME

THE lamps glow here and there, then echo down
The vast deserted vistas of the town—
Each light the echo'd note of some refrain
Repeated in the city's fevered brain.
Yet all is still, save when there wanders past
—Finding the silence of the night too long—
Some tattered wretch, who, from the night outcast,
Sings, with an aching heart, a comic song.
The vapid parrot-words flaunt through the night—
Silly and gay, yet terrible. We know
Men sang these words in many a deadly fight,
And threw them—laughing—to a solemn foe ;
Sang them where tattered houses stand up tall and
    stark,
And bullets whistle through the ruined street,
Where live men tread on dead men in the dark,
And skulls are sown in fields once sown with wheat.
Across the sea, where night is dark with blood
And rockets flash, and guns roar hoarse and deep,
They struggle through entanglements and mud,
They suffer wounds—and die—
                              But here they sleep.
From far away the outcast's vacuous song
Re-echoes like the singing of a throng ;
His dragging footfalls echo down the street,
And turn into a myriad marching feet.

December, 1916.

PEACE CELEBRATION

Now we can say of those who died unsung,
Unwept for, torn, " Thank God they were not blind
Or mad !   They've perished strong and young,
Missing the misery we elders find
In missing them."   With such a platitude
We try to cheer ourselves.   And for each life
Laid down for us, with duty well-imbued,
With song-on-lip, in splendid soldier strife—
For sailors, too, who willingly were sunk—
We'll shout " Hooray ! "—
                    And get a little drunk.

THE NEXT WAR

To SACHEVERELL

THE long war had ended.
Its miseries had grown faded.
Deaf men became difficult to talk to,
Heroes became bores.

Those alchemists,
Who had converted blood into gold,
Had grown elderly.
But they held a meeting,
Saying,
" We think perhaps we ought
To put up tombs
Or erect altars
To those brave lads
Who were so willingly burnt,
Or blinded,
Or maimed,
Who lost all likeness to a living thing,
Or were blown to bleeding patches of flesh
For our sakes.
It would look well.
Or we might even educate the children."
But the richest of these wizards
Coughed gently;
And he said,
" I have always been to the front
—In private enterprise—
I yield in public spirit
To no man.
I think yours is a very good idea

—A capital idea—
And not too costly.
But it seems to me
That the cause for which we fought
Is again endangered.
What more fitting memorial for the fallen
Than that their children
Should fall for the same cause ? "
Rushing eagerly into the street,
The kindly old gentlemen cried
To the young :
    " Will you sacrifice
    Through your lethargy
    What your fathers died to gain ?
    Our cause is in peril.
    The world must be made safe for the young!"
And the children
Went. . . .

Printed by Burleigh Ltd., at THE BURLEIGH PRESS, *Bristol*.

THE NEW READERS' LIBRARY

*Printed on thin paper, and bound in flexible
cloth. Size 7 × 4½ in. Price 3s. 6d. each.*

A new series of important copyright works by eminent
modern authors many of which have never before been
available at standard prices. The volumes, which will be
uniform in size, binding and price, have been specially
designed with the assistance of an expert printer and binder,
to meet the modern demand for handier books, without
sacrifice of the dignity and simplicity which are essential
to a good appearance on the shelves of a Library. Among
the authors whose works are included in the first list are —

Maurice Baring	William Gerhardi
Hilaire Belloc	W. H. Hudson
Augustine Birrell	Richard Jefferies
Edmund Blunden	Arthur Machen
David W. Bone	Edith Sitwell
James Oliver Curwood	Anton Tchekoff
Michael Fairless	H. M. Tomlinson

R. B. Cunninghame Graham

and arrangements are now being made for the inclusion of
many other works of equal value.

It will be noted that, while all the volumes are of high
literary standing, the Library is peculiarly rich in the
literature of the open-air, including such famous books
as W. H. Hudson's " Green Mansions " and " Birds and
Man," H. M. Tomlinson's " The Sea and the Jungle,"
Michael Fairless's " The Roadmender," Edmund Blunden's
" The Bonadventure " (a unique and too little known travel
book written in a modern spirit) and David Bone's sea yarn
" The Brassbounder." The same note is struck by such
novels as Hudson's " The Purple Land " and Richard
Jefferies " Amaryllis at the Fair."

FIRST LIST OF VOLUMES

1. GREEN MANSIONS

   A Romance of the Tropical Forest, by *W. H. Hudson.*

   An enthralling story of imaginative adventure in the tropical forest. The heroine, Rima, is famous everywhere owing to Mr. Epstein's sculpture of her in Hyde Park.

2. THE POLYGLOTS

   A Novel by *William Gerhardi,* author of " Futility."

   A story of the amorous adventures of a young man in cosmopolitan society, by the author of " Futility " : a very delicate record of what is really felt and thought about love by a young man and a girl. Full of humour, irony and satire.

3. THE SEA AND THE JUNGLE

   By *H. M. Tomlinson.* (Revised Edition.)

   A remarkable account of the sea and the jungle, unsurpassed in its truth to nature in the tropics and full of exciting incidents. " Entitles Mr. Tomlinson to a place in literature side by side with Joseph Conrad " (C.K.S.)

4. THE ROADMENDER

   By *Michael Fairless.*

   The beautiful vision of Life and Death which has brought joy and comfort to millions of men and women.

5. THE TERROR

A Fantasy, by *Arthur Machen*, author of "The Bowmen."

The haunting story of a terrible series of violent deaths in all parts of England and Wales; and the strange psychological cause of the epidemic. Mr. Machen, who has revised his book for this edition, has written nothing more eerie and more profound.

6. LOST DIARIES

By *Maurice Baring*.

Passages of unusual frankness from the lost diaries of Hamlet, Christopher Columbus, Mrs. John Milton, George Washington, Smith Minor, and many others give the reader a new insight into the more human, if less heroic, characteristics of many interesting people. A very clever and amusing skit.

7. THE BONADVENTURE

A Random Journal of an Atlantic Holiday, by *Edmund Blunden*.

The adventures of the famous modern poet as an amateur Purser on a cargo ship. A very original and vivid narrative of life on the sea and in South American ports. "A first-rate piece of work" (H. M. Tomlinson)

8. SUCCESS, AND OTHER SKETCHES

By *R. B. Cunninghame Graham*.

Seventeen tales of many countries, all inspired by his passionate love of country and country-folk, by the famous Scottish traveller.

9. BIRDS AND MAN
   By *W. H. Hudson*.
   The greatest of bird-lovers here pours out the treasures of his knowledge of English birds; the results of a lifetime of passionate observation.

10. THE BLACK MONK
    And other Stories by *Anton Tchekoff*. Translated, with an introduction by *R. E. C. Long*.
    Twelve stories by the author of " The Cherry Orchard," specially selected for their appeal to British readers.

11. GOD'S COUNTRY
    The Trail to Happiness, by *James Oliver Curwood*.
    How the author, a great hunter and killer, was converted by the beauty of Spring in the Canadian Rockies to fellowship with animals and nature— " the physical part of God " : an entrancing book of observation in the wilds.

12. BUCOLIC COMEDIES
    By *Edith Sitwell*.
    Truth and Beauty, fantasy and humour, are inextricably mixed in this favourite volume by the greatest woman poet of our times.

13. THE BRASSBOUNDER
    A Tale of the Sea, by *David W. Bone*.
    A strong full-blooded sea story, recording sixteen months of an apprentice's life on an old sailing ship between Glasgow and San Francisco, full of inimitable portraits of seamen and their perilous life.

14. THE PURPLE LAND
By W. H. Hudson.
Hudson's first book, "One Richard Lamb's adventures in the Banda Oriental in South America as told by himself." A magnificent romantic story, full of exciting incident.

15. CALIBAN'S GUIDE TO LETTERS AND LAMBKIN'S REMAINS
By *H. Belloc*.
These satirical accounts of Thomas Caliban, D.D., and J. A. Lambkin, M.A., and their works, provide the most amusing and instructive criticism of modern life and letters.

16 OBITER DICTA
By *Augustine Birrell*.
This volume contains both series of the inimitable essays on literary subjects which made Mr. Birrell's name a household word. Carlyle, Browning, Pope, Dr. Johnson, Lamb, Bookbuying are among the titles of the chapters.

17. AMARYLLIS AT THE FAIR
By *Richard Jefferies*.
" By ' Amaryllis at the Fair ' Jefferies stands among the half-dozen country writers of the nineteenth century whose work is racy of the English soil and of rural human nature. The scenes, the descriptions, the conversations are spontaneous as life " (Edward Garnett).

18. A CRYSTAL AGE
    By *W. H. Hudson.*
    A new utopia or vision of a more perfect future;
    Hudson's dream of the human race in a new forest
    period, inspired by his passionate love of trees and
    birds.

19. THE KISS AND OTHER STORIES
    By *Anton Tchekoff,* translated by *R. E. C.
    Long.*
    Fifteen more selected stories by the author of " The
    Cherry Orchard," who, beyond all others, has made
    Russian thought and Russian life intelligible to
    English readers.

20. GOSSIP OF THE SEVENTEENTH AND
    EIGHTEENTH CENTURIES
    Six studies in the human side of history, by
    John Beresford.
    Studies of famous men and women, founded upon
    private diaries and letters, more intimate and
    personal than appear in formal histories.

Also in PREPARATION

21 FUTILITY
    A Novel, by *William Gerhardi.*

22. TRIPLE FUGUE. Stories.
    By *Osbert Sitwell.*

23. EL OMBÚ By *W. H. Hudson.*

24. SIX SHORT PLAYS. By *John Galsworthy.*

THE READERS' LIBRARY

A series of copyright books of individual merit and permanent value. Full-size library editions. Crown 8vo. ($7\frac{1}{2} \times 5$ in.). Bound in cloth. 3s. 6d. net each.

"This admirably produced and serviceable series."—THE OUTLOOK.

LIST OF VOLUMES

CONFESSIONS OF A LITTLE MAN DURING GREAT DAYS. By LEONID ANDREYEF.

AVRIL. By HILAIRE BELLOC. Essays on the Poetry of the French Renaissance.

OBITER DICTA. By the Rt. Hon. AUGUSTINE BIRRELL, K.C.

MEMOIRS OF A SURREY LABOURER. By GEORGE BOURNE.

THE BETTESWORTH BOOK. By GEORGE BOURNE.

LUCY BETTESWORTH. By GEORGE BOURNE.

CHANGE IN THE VILLAGE. By GEORGE BOURNE.

STUDIES IN POETRY. By STOPFORD A. BROOKE, M.A., LL.D.

COMPARATIVE STUDIES IN NURSERY RHYMES. By LINA ECKENSTEIN.

TWENTY-SIX MEN AND A GIRL. Stories by MAXIM GORKY.

VILLA RUBEIN, AND OTHER STORIES. By JOHN GALSWORTHY.

HOPE, AND OTHER SKETCHES. By R. B. CUNNINGHAME GRAHAM.

BROUGHT FORWARD. Sketches by R. B. CUNNINGHAME GRAHAM.

A HATCHMENT. Sketches by R. B. CUNNINGHAME GRAHAM.

EL OMBÚ. By W. H. HUDSON.

A CRYSTAL AGE. A Romance of the Future. By W. H. HUDSON.

GREEN MANSIONS. A Romance. By W. H. HUDSON.

THE PURPLE LAND. A Narrative of Adventure. By W. H. HUDSON.

THE READERS' LIBRARY

GERALD DUCKWORTH & CO., LTD.
3 HENRIETTA STREET, LONDON, W.C.2